Grandma Margie's
Courageous Tale:
David and the Giant

Dr. K.T. Zulkowski

Published by Mz. Kim Productions
4263 Tierra Rejada Rd #151
Moorpark, CA 93021
www.mzkimproductions.com

ISBN: 978-1-962106-02-3

Printed in United States of America
First Printing: August 2023
Date of Copyright: July 5,2023
Edited by Joshua Nickel

For permissions, please contact: Mz. Kim Productions
4263 Tierra Rejada Rd #151
Moorpark, CA 93021
www.mzkimproductions.com
mzkimproductions@gmail.com

Dedication:

This book is dedicated to all the children and families around the world, who are embarking on this enchanting journey with Grandma Margie. It is my sincerest hope that these pages will serve as a source of joy, inspiration, and lasting memories for each and every one of you.

To the children, who possess an innate curiosity and a boundless imagination, may this book ignite your sense of wonder and encourage you to explore the world with open minds and open hearts. May you find solace in its pages, discovering the timeless lessons of humility, trust, and the power of unity.

To the families, who are the pillars of love and support in these young lives, may this book strengthen the bonds that hold you together. May it serve as a reminder of the importance of family, and the joy that comes from sharing stories, laughter, and precious moments. May it inspire you to create cherished memories and traditions that will be passed down through generations.

As we embark on this adventure with Grandma Margie, let us remember that it is not just a journey for grandchildren, but for all children and families. Regardless of age or relation, the lessons and experiences within these pages are meant to be shared and cherished by everyone.

May this book be a beacon of hope, reminding us all to trust in God's plans and to spread love and kindness wherever we may go. May it remind us of the power of storytelling, and the ability of words to heal, inspire, and transform.

With heartfelt gratitude and warmest wishes,

Dr. K.T. Zulkowski

Author's Note:

I am thrilled to present "Grandma Margie's Courageous Tale: David and the Giant" to readers of all ages. This story holds a special place in my heart, as it is inspired by the incredible courage and determination of my own grandmother, Margie.

Growing up, I would often spend summers with my grandmother, listening to her captivating stories. She had a unique way of bringing Bible stories to life, infusing them with her own experiences and wisdom. One tale that always stood out was the story of David and Goliath.

In "Grandma Margie's Courageous Tale: David and the Giant," I have taken the essence of my grandmother's storytelling and woven it into a narrative that combines faith, bravery, and the power of believing in oneself. Through this story, I hope to ignite the imagination and inspire readers to face their own giants with courage and determination.

While the characters and events in this book are fictional, they are grounded in the timeless teachings of the Bible. I have aimed to stay true to the spirit of the original story while adding my own creative touches to make it accessible and engaging for modern readers.
I must express my gratitude to my grandmother, Margie, for instilling in me a love for storytelling and a deep appreciation for the lessons found in the Bible. Her unwavering faith and resilience continue to inspire me every day.

Lastly, I would like to extend my heartfelt thanks to all the readers who have joined me on this journey. It is my hope that "Grandma Margie's Courageous Tale: David and the Giant" will entertain, encourage, and uplift you as you embark on this adventure with David and his giant. May the story remind us all of the power that lies within, waiting to be unleashed when we face our fears head-on.

With love and gratitude,

Dr. K.T. Zulkowski

Educational Value:

This book not only aims to entertain and captivate young readers, but also provides numerous educational benefits that can enhance their learning and development. Here are some of the educational values embedded within the pages of this book:

1. Language Development: Through engaging storytelling, children are exposed to rich vocabulary, sentence structures, and descriptive language. This helps expand their vocabulary, improve their reading comprehension, and develop their own storytelling and writing skills.

2. Cultural Awareness: As Grandma Margie embarks on her global adventures, children are introduced to different cultures, traditions, and landmarks from around the world. This promotes cultural awareness, sensitivity, and understanding, fostering a sense of global citizenship.

3. Geography and History: Each destination Grandma Margie visits provides an opportunity to learn about the geography, history, and landmarks of various countries and regions. Children can expand their knowledge of different countries, continents, and historical events, sparking their curiosity and broadening their understanding of the world.

4. Moral Lessons: Throughout the book, Grandma Margie encounters various challenges and learns important life lessons. Children can learn about the values of perseverance, friendship, compassion, and forgiveness, as well as the consequences of actions. These moral lessons help instill positive character traits and empathy in young readers.

5. Problem-Solving Skills: As Grandma Margie navigates through different situations and obstacles, children are encouraged to think critically and develop problem-solving skills. They can analyze the characters' actions and decisions, predicting outcomes and considering alternative solutions.

6. Creativity and Imagination: This book sparks the imagination, inviting children to visualize the vivid descriptions and settings. It encourages creative thinking and inspires children to create their own stories, drawings, and imaginative play.

7. Emotional Intelligence: Through the emotional journey of Grandma Margie, children can develop their emotional intelligence by identifying and understanding different emotions and their impact on relationships. This helps them develop empathy and emotional resilience.

8. Family Bonding: The stories in this book provide an opportunity for families to bond and share quality time together. Reading aloud, discussing the stories, and engaging in related activities can strengthen familial relationships and create lasting memories.

By incorporating these educational values, this book aims to not only entertain but also educate young readers, fostering their love for learning and nurturing their intellectual, emotional, and social development.

Grandma Margie's
Courageous Tale:
David and the Giant

Dr. K.T. Zulkowski

In a cozy living room, Grandma Margie gathered
her grandchildren Zipporah and Zion to share
an incredible story from the Bible. They
snuggled up on the couch, ready to embark
on a courageous journey through the story of
David and the giant.

"Listen closely, my dear ones," Grandma Margie said, opening her Bible. "This is a story of faith, bravery, and how God can help us overcome any giant in our lives."

"Long ago, in the land of Israel, there was a young shepherd boy named David," Grandma Margie began. "He was chosen by God to become a great king."

"David spent his days tending to his father's sheep," Grandma Margie explained. "He loved God deeply and would often play his harp, singing songs of praise and worship."

"One day, a giant named Goliath challenged the Israelite army," Grandma Margie continued. "He was a fearsome warrior, and no one dared to face him."

"But David, filled with faith and trust in God, volunteered to fight Goliath," Grandma Margie said. "He knew that with God by his side, he could conquer any giant."

"David approached Goliath with only a sling and five smooth stones," Grandma Margie explained. "He knew that his strength came from God, not from weapons or armor."

"With a single stone, David struck Goliath in the forehead, and the giant fell to the ground," Grandma Margie said. "God had given David the victory, showing that faith and courage can overcome any obstacle."

The Israelite army rejoiced,
and David became a hero,"
Grandma Margie continued.
"He went on to become a great
king, always remembering that
it was God who gave him the
strength to face the giant."

Zipporah and Zion listened intently, their hearts filled with awe and inspiration. They understood that just like David, they too could face their own giants with faith in God.

And so, Grandma Margie's courageous tale of David and the giant came to an end. Zipporah and Zion felt empowered, knowing that God would always be with them, helping them face any challenges that came their way.

www.ingramcontent.com/pod-product-compliance
Lightning Source LLC
Chambersburg PA
CBHW040513150626
46551CB00033B/2640